YOU CAN BE A WOMAN CARDIOLOGIST

Rita F. Redberg
and
Judith Love Cohen

Illustrations:
David A. Katz

Editing:
Janice J. Martin

Cascade Pass, Inc.

Copyright © 1996 by Cascade Pass, Inc.
Published by Cascade Pass, Inc., Suite 235, 10734 Jefferson Blvd.
Culver City CA 90230-4969
Printed by Gemini Graphics, Marina Del Rey, CA
All rights reserved.
First Edition 1996
You Can Be a Woman Cardiologist was written by Rita F. Redberg and Judith Love Cohen, designed and illustrated by David Katz, and edited by Janice Martin.
This book is one of a series that emphasizes the value of science and mathematical studies by depicting real women whose careers provide inspirational role models. Other books in the series include:

You Can Be A Woman Engineer   *You Can Be A Woman Egyptologist*
You Can Be A Woman Architect   *You Can Be A Woman Paleontologist*
You Can Be A Woman Marine Biologist *You Can Be A Woman Astronomer*
You Can Be A Woman Zoologist   *You Can Be A Woman Oceanographer*

Library of Congress Cataloging-in-Publication Data

Redberg, Rita F. (Rita Fran), 1956-
    You can be a woman cardiologist/ Rita F. Redberg and Judith Love Cohen ; illustrations, David A. Katz .
        p.   cm.
    Summary: The author describes how she decided to become a doctor and the work she does as a cardiologist
    ISBN 1-880599-18-X (pbk.)
        1. Cardiology--Vocational guidance--Juvenile literature.   2. Women physicians --Vocational guidance--Juvenile literature.   [1. Redberg, Rita F. (Rita Fran), 1956- . 2. Cardiologists.   3. Physicians.   4. Women--Biography.   5. Occupations.]
 I. Cohen, Judith Love, 1933- . II. Katz, David A. (David Arthur),   1949-   . III. Title.
   RC669.R38   1996   96-8865
   616.1' 2 ' 023--dc20
                                                                         CIP
                                                                          AC

Dedication

This book is dedicated by Rita Redberg to her husband David who supports her in everything she does, and to Anna and Rebecca who give her so much joy.

And this book is also dedicated by Rita Redberg to her parents, Sam and Mae, whose love and encouragement and confidence in her ability helped her to realize that women could do anything.

And this book is also dedicated by Rita Redberg to her many men and women colleagues and friends who help to make it all fun.

This book is also dedicated by Judith Love Cohen to Dr. Robert Nankin, her cardiologist, who encouraged her to take the subject matter "to heart" and choose a more active and lower fat lifestyle.

The noise of the Lear Jet's engines seemed very loud to Dr. Redberg's ears. Normally she would read or do paperwork on a short plane ride, but this time she was on edge. Although she was aware of the spectacular sunrise over the eastern seaboard, she was focused on returning to the hospital.

In New York there was a relatively young man dying of heart failure. His chances of survival did not look good, until . . . Dr. Redberg glanced over at the styrofoam container, something that resembles an ice bucket. That "ice bucket" contains this young man's last hope.

Rita Redberg has just come from a hospital in Atlanta, Georgia, where her team helped "harvest" the heart of a donor, another young man who died in a motorcycle accident and whose family chose to help someone else have a chance at life with a new heart.

The container is keeping the donor heart cold and alive until they get it back to Presbyterian Hospital in New York. Dr. Redberg is part of a team that will transplant this heart into the waiting patient.

This type of operation is relatively new; the first heart transplant was done in 1967. Today, doctors know more about preventing the body from rejecting a new heart. To the patient, this new life-saving heart will be seen as foreign, and the body's defenses will want to treat it as an invading virus, causing it to wither and die. Today, doctors use drugs to prevent this rejection, and transplant patients are living more than ten years after surgery.

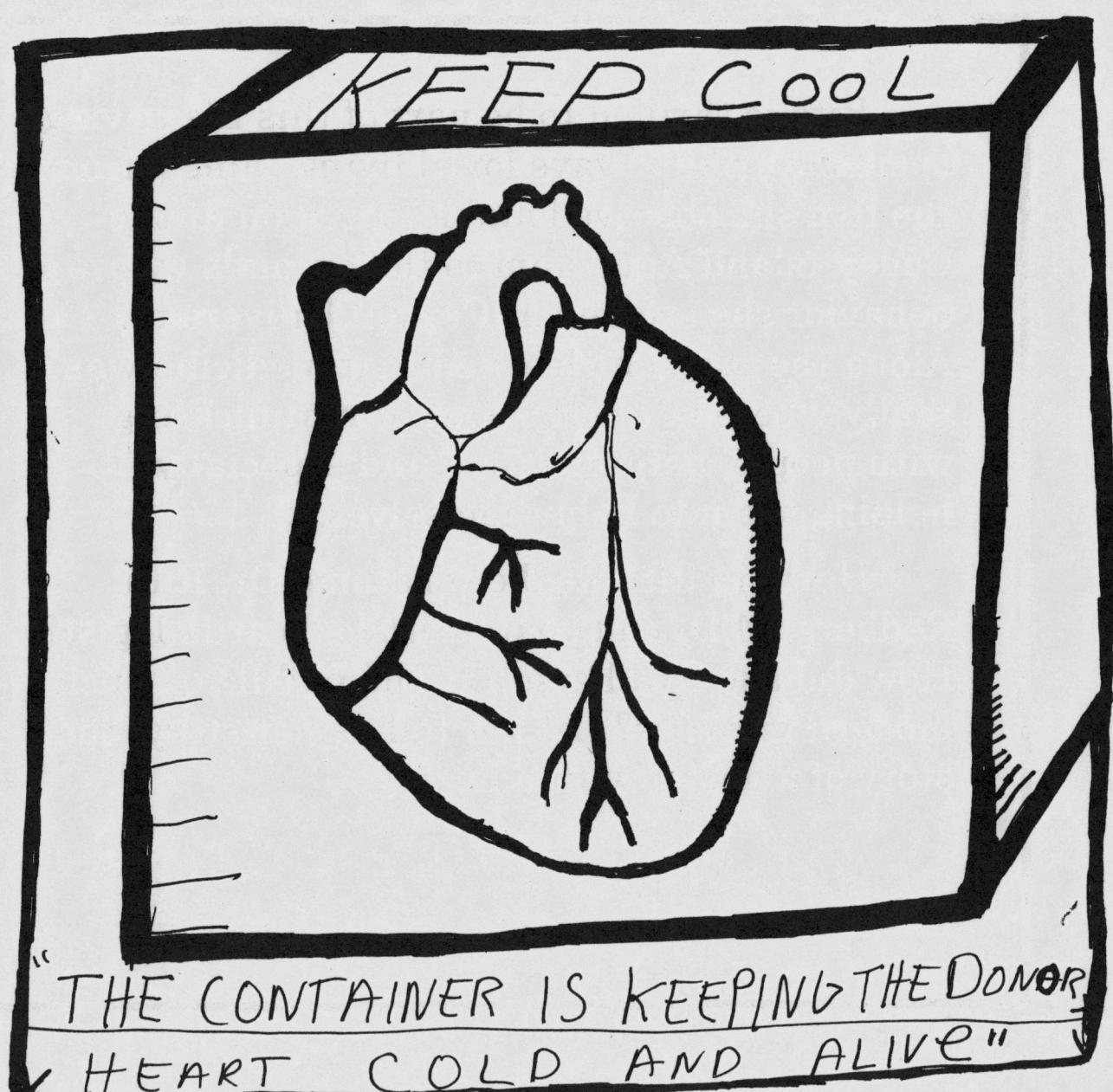

Rita is thrilled to be part of this life-saving operation. She always loved living things, from the fish she observed and lectured on at the Coney Island Aquarium to the animals whose behavior she studied at Cornell University. Along the way, she learned that medicine was really where her heart was: communicating with people, helping them, and especially helping them to help themselves.

How did Rita Redberg become Dr. Rita Redberg, M.D. and board-certified cardiologist? How did she find herself in the middle of such modern miracles? Let her tell us her story, the story of a doctor with a heart . . .

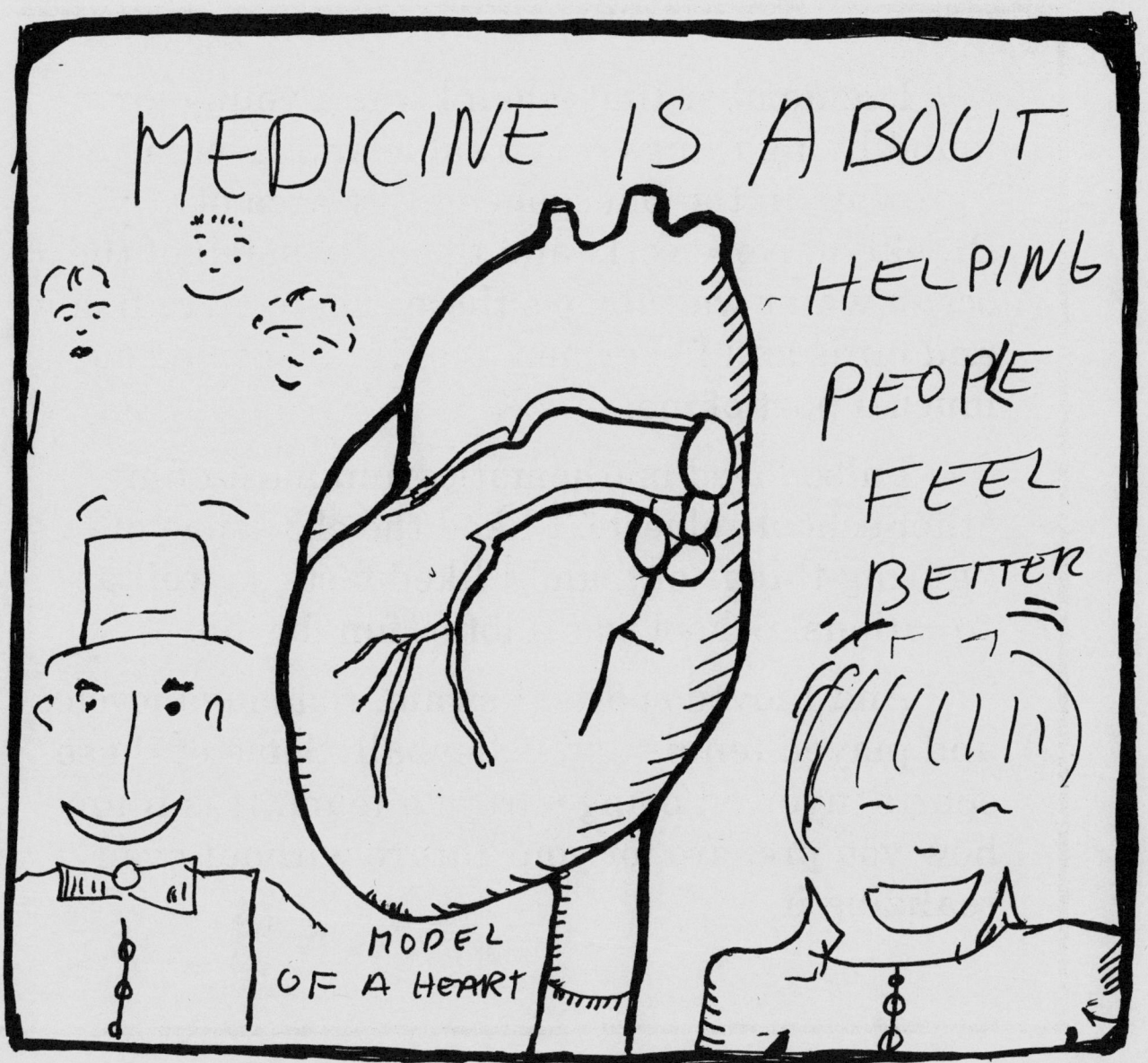

I remember that when I was a young girl I found living things remarkable and fascinating. I grew up in the Sheepshead Bay area of Brooklyn, New York, and the salty smell of the ocean water was always there. There were fish and birds and fishermen, too. It all seemed so much a part of me.

I also loved mathematics and most of my other school subjects. I liked the challenge of figuring things out, and I liked facts as well as equations. School was a lot of fun for me.

And I loved sports. I swam, rode my bicycle, and played tennis and volleyball. Some of these sports involved being part of a team. It is funny how you prepare for your future without even realizing it.

When I was in high school I worked on the school paper, and I thought I would be a journalist for the New York Times. Journalism seemed so objective, so factual.

But I had two important experiences while I was in high school that showed me a different path. I became a volunteer lecturer at the Coney Island Aquarium where I studied the creatures of the sea and learned of the strange and wonderful ways they had of adapting to their world. This reawakened my love for all living things. Then I participated in a program called "Classroom Without Walls" where we went out into the community to study and observe. I worked at the Greenpoint Hospital and realized that people were even more interesting than fish because people could talk to you!

I was going to study medicine.

In college I majored in biology. I learned about the wonders of the human body: the skeleton, the digestive system, and the circulatory system. These are the structures and systems that bring food and oxygen to the parts of the body and support its growth and functioning.

<u>Skeleton</u>: the inner scaffolding or frame. Consists of bones that protect (e.g., skull, ribs) and bones that move (e.g., arms, legs, joints).

<u>Energy systems</u>: food and oxygen are fuel. Consists of digestive system, circulatory system (e.g., heart, blood cells) and respiratory system (e.g., lungs, nose).

<u>Motor and nervous systems</u>: from impulse to motion. Consists of muscles that move, nerves that transmit the message to move and the all-important brain to motivate and coordinate the motion.

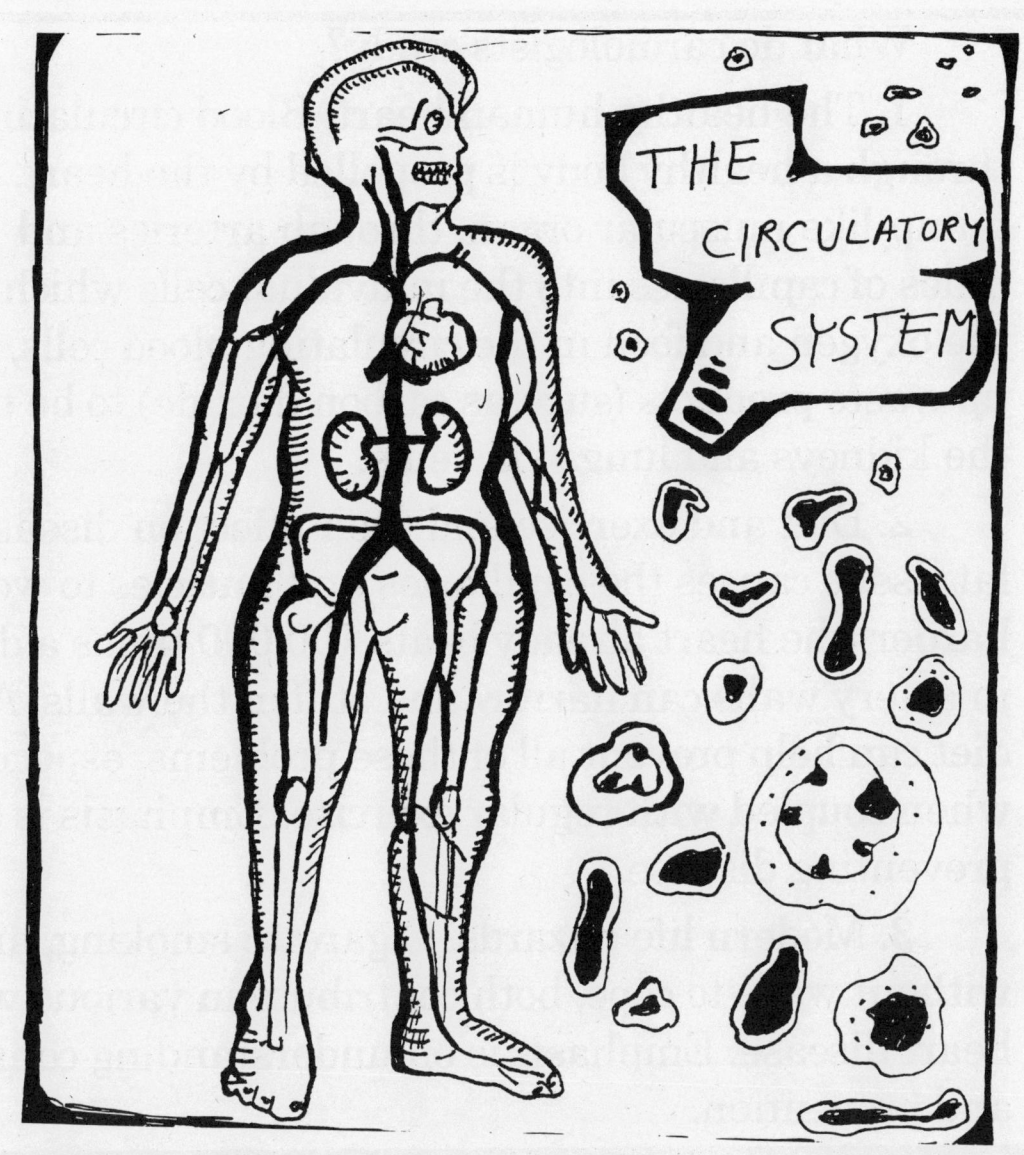

What do cardiologists study?

1. The healthy human heart. Blood circulating through a healthy body is propelled by the heart, a pump-like muscular organ, through arteries and 15,000 miles of capillaries into the individual cells which take up the oxygen and food in the circulating blood cells, and give up waste products (such as carbon dioxide) to be taken to the kidneys and lungs via veins.

2. Diet and exercise and their effect on disease. Extra fat tissue causes the capillaries and muscles to work harder (the heart already beats 100,000 times a day); fats in artery walls can narrow and stiffen the walls. A good diet can help prevent all of these problems, especially when coupled with regular exercise. Emphasis is on preventing disease.

3. Modern life hazards. Cigarette smoking, and stress without ways to cope, both contribute in various ways to heart disease. Emphasis is on understanding connections and prevention.

How do doctors work? Medicine is both an art and a science. Doctors can see two patients with the same blood pressure, heart rate, and height and weight, and one can be cheerful, happy and healthy while the other might be depressed, unhappy and ultimately unhealthy.

Medicine is a healing art, and doctors depend a lot on human communication; i.e., communication to earn trust so that patients will tell you important things and make the changes you want them to make, and communication so that the patient can understand how to get better faster.

Cardiologists have a lot of tools and instruments to help them: from simple things like stethoscopes to listen to the heart and lungs, sphygmomanometers (blood pressure cuffs) to measure blood pressure, and a watch with a second hand to count a pulse, to more complicated instruments like electrocardiographs which diagram the electrical complexities of the heartbeat, lipid profiles that measure levels of different types of blood cholesterol, and ultrasound machines that get detailed pictures of the heart.

Now that I knew what cardiologists did, I had to learn how to do it. First I studied medicine, then internal medicine, and finally I received more specialized training and research to become a board-certified cardiologist.

I'm particularly pleased that I've been able to participate in some exciting research studies. One of those studies concerns cardiac risk factors in older women. Cardiac risk is the danger of having a heart attack or getting heart disease. Doctors measure things in people who seem healthy and then see which patients get sick and which ones don't. That is how we discovered that smoking, diet and exercise levels have a relationship with heart disease. Doctors can have patients run on a treadmill while they take pictures of the heart at the same time to see how the heart reacts to stress. We can take blood tests and do various other measurements. Mostly, doctors have studied heart disease in men. I felt fortunate to have the opportunity to conduct this kind of research on women to see if our risk factors are different than those for men.

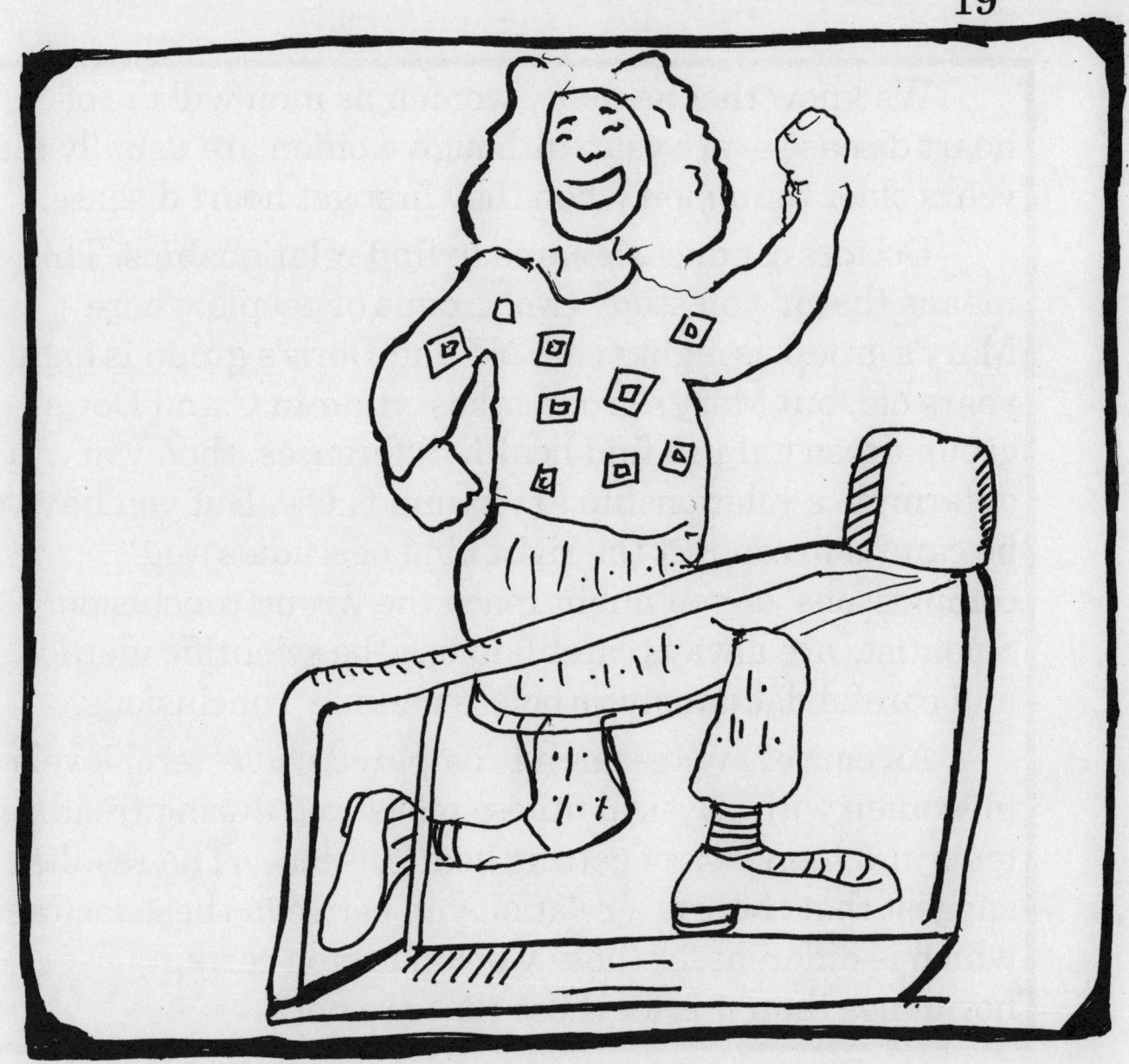

We know that as many women as men will die of heart disease every year, although women are usually ten years older than men when they first get heart disease.

Doctors conduct research to find relationships. This means that if you study two groups of people where Mary's group is eight years old and Doris's group is eight years old, but Mary's group takes vitamin C and Doris's group doesn't, if you find health differences, then you can determine a relationship to vitamin C use. But you have to be careful to conduct the right kind of studies and comparisons, or you might reach the wrong conclusion. Scientists are always careful to use the scientific method and careful data analysis before making conclusions.

As part of my research I compared cholesterol levels in women with physical fitness measured during treadmill tests and their risk of getting heart disease. The results suggest that there is a relationship between these factors which is different for those women taking certain hormones than it is for those that are not.

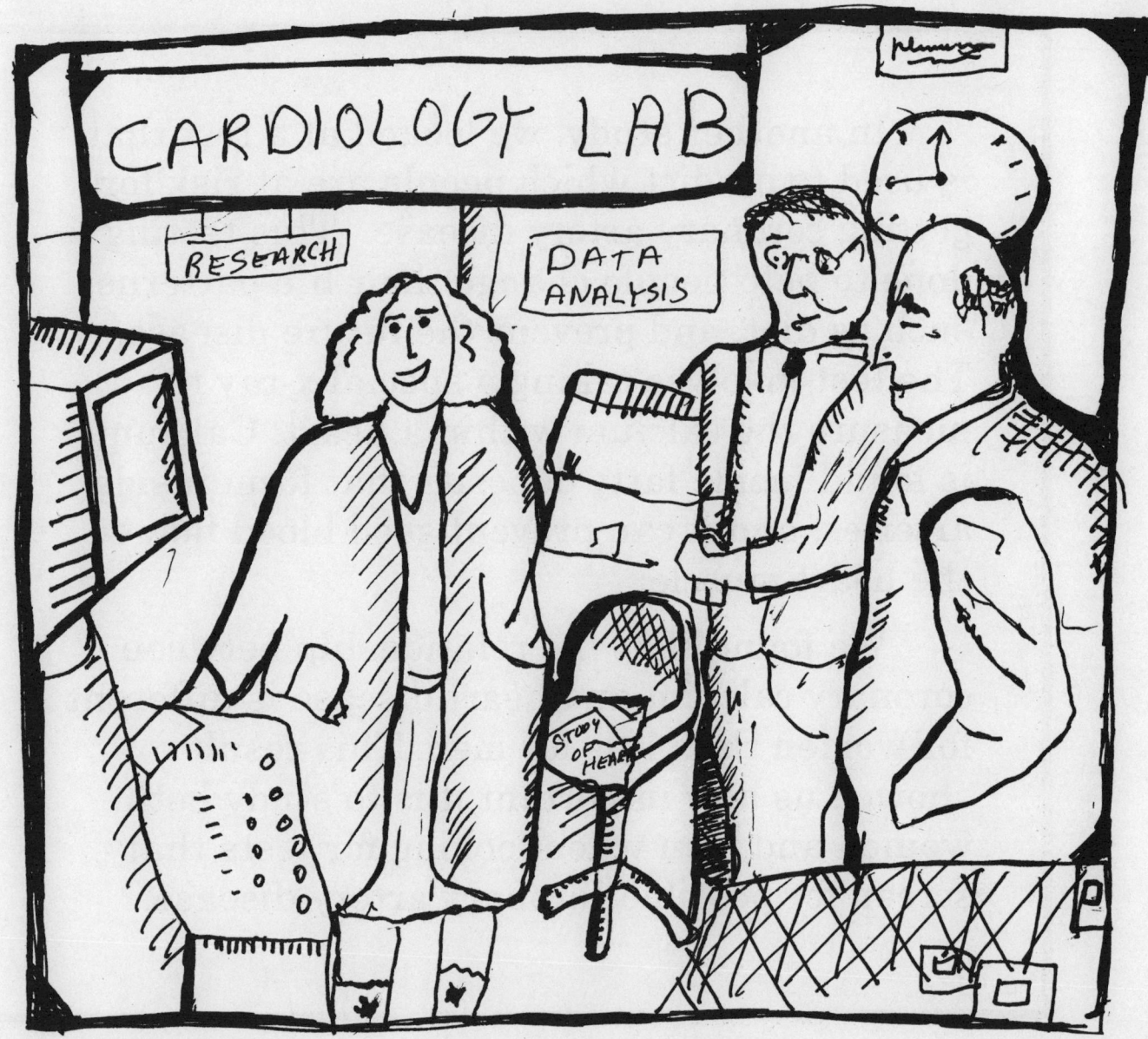

In another study, we looked at a test that is used to predict which people are at risk for getting coronary artery disease. This testing is done to help people change their life patterns, such as diet, and prevent the future disease. The test involves taking a special x-ray to measure the calcium within a heart. Calcium is found inside fatty deposits that form inside arteries, and it can prevent good blood flow to the heart muscle.

We found that the relationship between coronary calcium and heart disease is different for women than it is for men. This result showed us how important it is to study both women and men when looking for tests that screen for possible coronary artery disease.

Today, I work at a hospital located within a major university that also has a school of medicine. This way, I can both teach and see patients. A typical day at work might begin with a meeting about health policy. I try to solve problems related to the cost of future medical care and how to use our resources to provide care for people.

Next, I may have a conference call with colleagues from the American Heart Association to plan a speaker for our next meeting on Women in Cardiology. Then I might have a staff meeting with my assistants to review the effectiveness of tests and treatments for our heart patients and to ensure that what we're doing is really helping them.

Next, I might review procedures. I look at ultrasound pictures of a heart in the Echocardiography Lab. My interpretion of the images can help other doctors care for people with heart disease.

Finally, I may see patients in my office who have had heart attacks or heart failure. As a cardiologist, being able to do lots of different things in one day is very exciting!

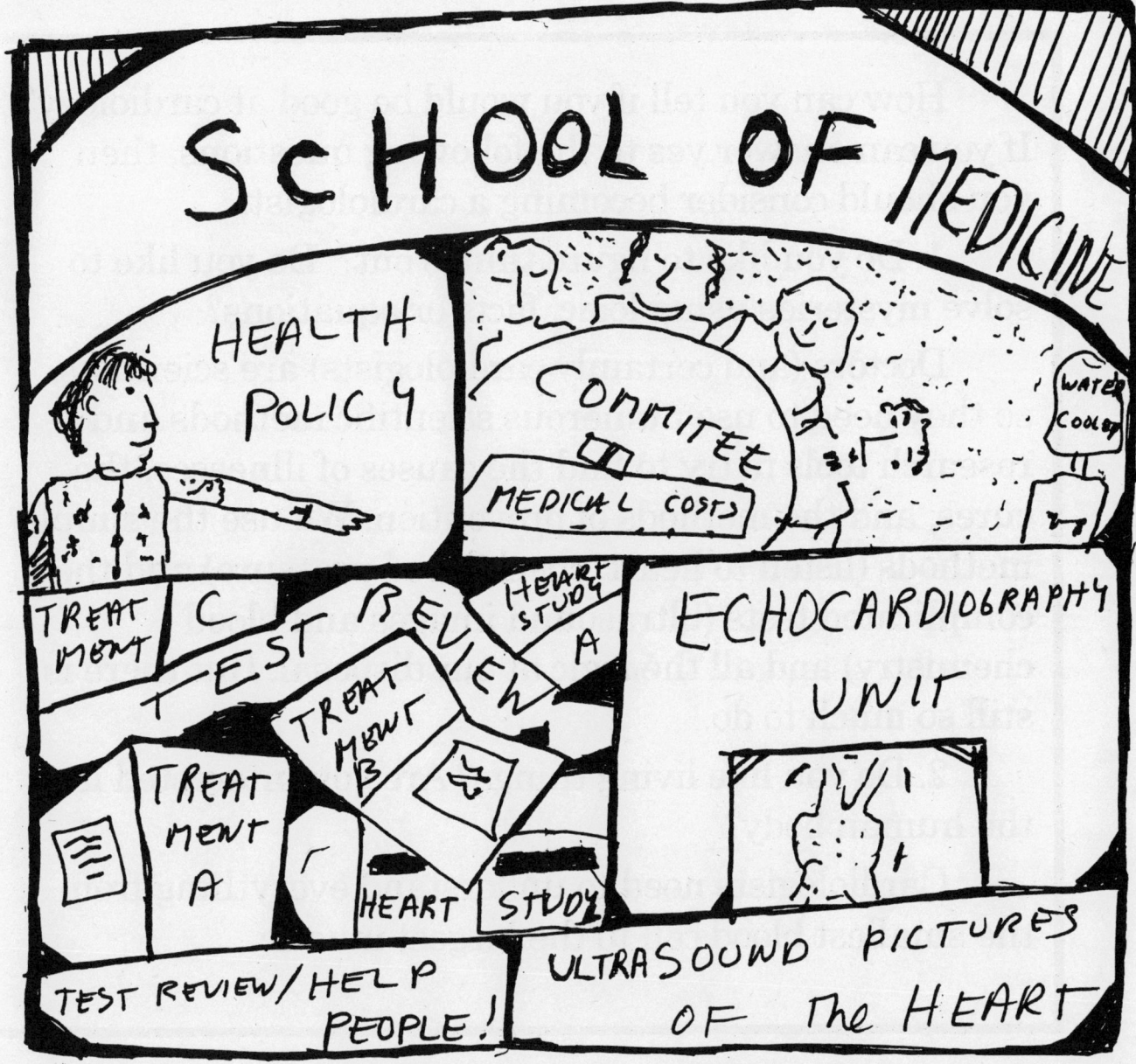

How can you tell if you would be good at cardiology? If you can answer yes to the following questions, then you should consider becoming a cardiologist.

1. Do you like to figure things out? Do you like to solve mysteries using logic, facts or equations?

Doctors (and certainly cardiologists) are scientists, so they need to use numerous scientific methods and research tools to try to find the causes of illnesses, the cures, and the methods of prevention. We use the simple methods (listen to heart, check blood pressure) and the complicated tests (ultrasound images and blood chemistry) and all the logic at our disposal. But there is still so much to do.

2. Do you like living things? Are you interested in the human body?

Cardiologists need to understand everything from the smallest blood cell to the largest muscle.

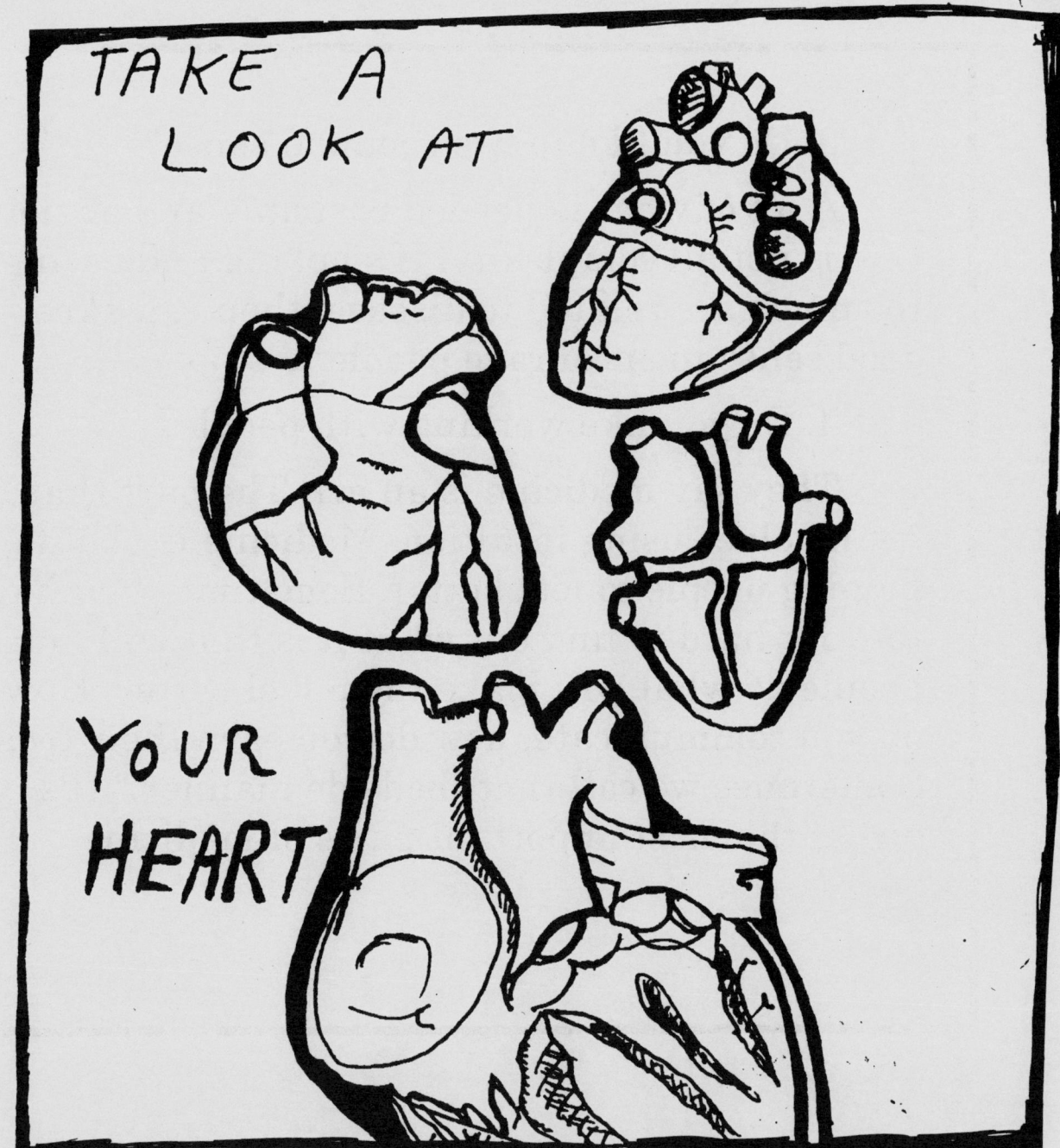

3. Do you like to use common sense?

A lot of what is needed is simple and obvious. Life is not all complexity. If smoking and eating too much are related to disease, then it makes good sense to encourage people to stop.

4. Do you like working with people?

They say medicine is an art. The part that is art involves using intuition. Medicine is about helping people to feel better. Sometimes you have to work hard to find out what it is that will help people do what will make them feel better. How do you communicate, how do you earn their trust? Sometimes we call that "bedside manner." It's one of the most important parts of medicine.

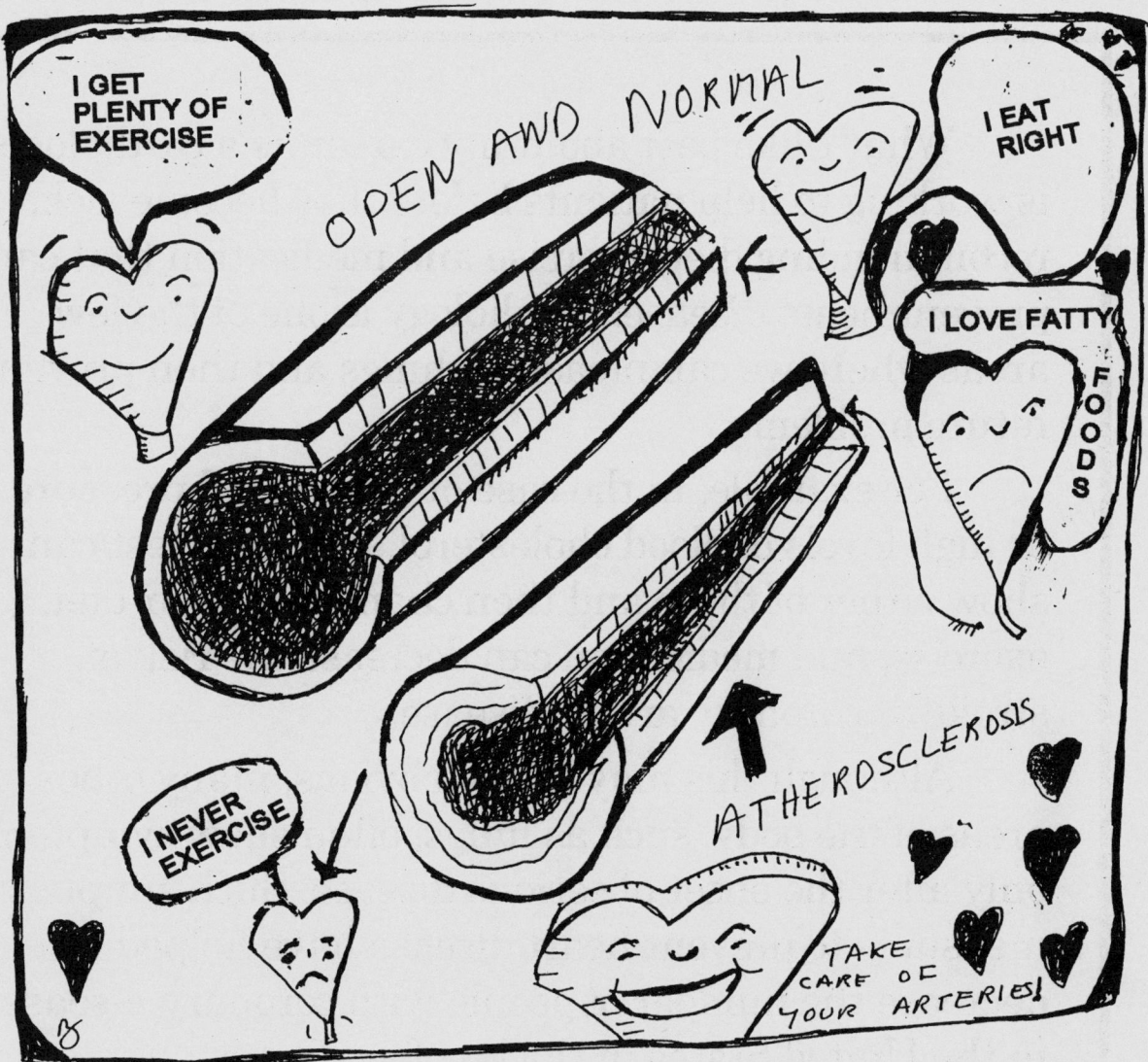

What I like best about my career as a cardiologist is working to help patients before they become sick, recommending diet, exercise and medication that can prevent heart disease. Cardiology is one of the few areas where we can measure things and then prevent future problems.

For example, in the case of high blood pressure or high levels of blood cholesterol, a simple test can show either of these and then changes in your diet, exercise, and medication can decrease the risk of stroke or coronary artery disease.

Although this may sound obvious, many other areas of the body, such as lungs, often show symptoms only after the onset of serious disease. Such simple measures to prevent heart disease have helped decrease the number of people with coronary disease in the United States in the last few decades.

My future goals are to continue my research and administrative duties at my teaching hospital, while also continuing to see patients so that I stay in touch with the reality of what cardiology is all about.

And I want to continue to ride my bicycle and play tennis. (I practice what I preach to my patients. Exercise is very important!)

And I care passionately about the future. I want my children to grow up not only healthy, but also secure that the rewarding aspects of life that we currently enjoy will be there for them in the future: health care, education, museums and symphonies. I want all people to be able to have a certain "quality" to their life that involves more than just living longer.

If you want to understand: how the heart muscle pumps blood through a body; how to encourage people to learn ways to keep their hearts healthier; how to find the relationship between various factors involved in heart disease and how to use the complicated and the simple instruments for measuring the heart; how to communicate with staff, committee members, and the public about health care details of today and the future discoveries of tomorrow; and how to use technology, from heart transplants to understanding diet, from ultrasound images to counting a pulse, then you can do it too. You can be a woman cardiologist.

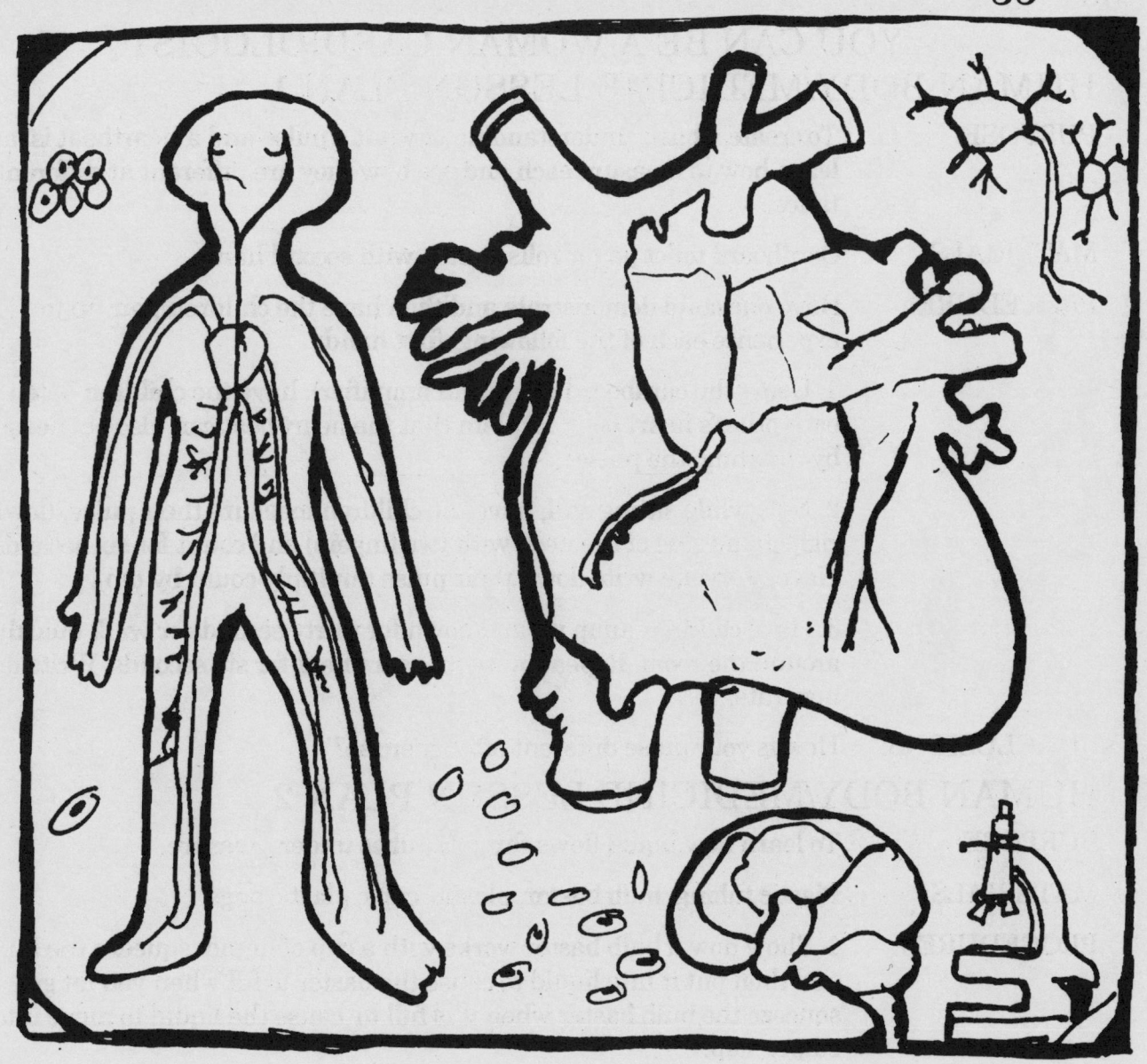

YOU CAN BE A WOMAN CARDIOLOGIST
HUMAN BODY/MEDICINE LESSON PLAN 1

PURPOSE: To create a basic understanding of what a pulse and a heartbeat is, and to learn how to measure each and see how they are different at different times.

MATERIALS: Cardboard toilet paper rolls, watch with second hand.

PROCEDURE: Have one child demonstrate and then have the children pair up to experience each of the following, first hand:

1. Using the cardboard roll (as an amplifier), have the children listen to each other's heart beat. Explain that the heart beat can also be measured by counting the pulse.

2. Now while sitting still, have the children measure their pulse, (lower right-hand side of the neck with two fingers) and count for six seconds. Have everyone write down their pulse (multiply count by ten).

3. Have children jump up and down for thirty seconds or walk quickly around the room. Repeat pulse measurement for six seconds. Write down new rate.

CONCLUSIONS: How is your pulse different after exercise?

HUMAN BODY/MEDICINE LESSON PLAN 2

PURPOSE: To learn how liquid flows through tubes under pressure.

MATERIALS: Plastic tubing, bulb baster, plastic cups, plastic bags.

PROCEDURES:

1. Show how a bulb baster works with a cup of liquid: squeeze the bulb and then put it into liquid to cause the baster to fill when you let go; squeeze the bulb baster when it is full to cause the liquid to move into an empty cup.

2. With plastic tube and two cups, place each end of the plastic tube in each cup. Show how water seeks its own level by moving the cups up and down next to each other.

CONCLUSIONS: What is the role of pressure in moving liquid?

HUMAN BODY/MEDICINE LESSON PLAN 3

PURPOSE: To develop an understanding of the workings of the heart and other parts of the circulatory system.

MATERIALS: Clay, paint, construction paper, plastic tubing, rubber or cork plugs or stoppers.

PROCEDURES: 1. Have the children draw a picture of the four chambers of the heart and show how the blood moves from one chamber to another.

2. Have the children build a model of the heart out of clay or paper. Put heart openings with plugs or stoppers at the points where the heart connects with the main arteries and veins. Have them add tubes at the end of these plugs. and describe where they will go.

CONCLUSIONS: How many heart beats does it take for a full cycle of filling and emptying the four heart chambers?

Where does the blood go?

How is the blood returning to the heart different from the blood leaving the heart.

RESOURCES: Library books with pictures and charts of the heart.

About the Authors:

Dr. Rita F. Redberg, a board-certified cardiovascular specialist, is concurrently an Assistant Clinical Professor of Medicine and Anesthesia, an Assistant Director of the Echocardiography Laboratory and a Co-Director for Women's Health Access, at the University of California, San Francisco Medical Center. Prior to this, she received her M.D. from the University of Pennsylvania School of Medicine and her bachelor's degree in biology from Cornell University in Ithaca New York. Dr. Redberg had extensive post-graduate training in internal medicine and cardiology in New York and in San Francisco. She has received many honors from her peers and from her community: the American Board of Internal Medicine invited her to write cardiology board questions and UCSF commended her for outstanding patient care. She heads a national committee of the American Heart Association on "Women in Cardiology," is on the editorial board of several major cardiology journals and has written and spoken extensively on the subject of women and health (also the subject of some of her research projects). She has also found the time to work with Medical Explorers (high school age) and provide mentoring for UCSF house staff. Among her nonacademic interests are bicycling (century rides) and tennis and, of course, her family. Dr. Redberg lives in San Francisco with her husband and two daughters.

Judith Love Cohen is a Registered Professional Electrical Engineer with bachelor's and master's degrees in engineering from the University of Southern California and University of California, Los Angeles. She has written plays, screenplays, and newspaper articles in addition to her series of children's books that began with *You Can Be a Woman Engineer*.

About the Illustrator:

David Arthur Katz received his training in art education and holds a master's degree from the University of South Florida. He is a credentialed teacher in the Los Angeles Unified School District. His involvement in the arts has encompassed animation, illustration, and playwriting, poetry and songwriting.